Th[illegible]

According to Luke

STUDY GUIDE

Jerome Kodell, O.S.B.

Little Rock Scripture Study

THE LITURGICAL PRESS

St. John's Abbey
Collegeville, Minnesota 56321

Office of the Bishop

DIOCESE OF LITTLE ROCK
2415 North Tyler Street
P.O. Box 7239, Forest Park Station
LITTLE ROCK, ARKANSAS 72217

Telephone
Area Code 501
664-0340

Dear Friend,

We Catholics have always believed that the Lord is present in his Word, in his sacrament, and through baptism and confirmation in each one of us. In post-Vatican II times, the emphasis upon Jesus in his Word among us has grown and deepened. In many parts of our country, Scripture study programs have become effective instruments for the deepening of our spiritual life.

Some years ago I encouraged our people to embrace God's holy Word. I used the words of Our Lord to St. Augustine, "Take and read." I asked that the Scriptures be prayerfully read. The Little Rock Scripture Study Program provided the way. Out of this program has come an enrichment of our spiritual life and a deeper and closer relationship to the Lord.

The pages of this study guide lay down the challenge to you, the reader. The Word of God can take root in your soul; the Word of God can change your life. The Word of God can make you a saint.

Your friend,

+ Andrew J. McDonald

✠Andrew J. McDonald
Bishop of Little Rock

Sacred Scripture

"The Church has always venerated the divine Scriptures just as she venerates the body of the Lord, since from the table of both the word of God and of the body of Christ she unceasingly receives and offers to the faithful the bread of life, especially in the sacred liturgy. She has always regarded the Scriptures together with sacred tradition as the supreme rule of faith, and will ever do so. For, inspired by God and committed once and for all to writing, they impart the word of God Himself without change, and make the voice of the Holy Spirit resound in the words of the prophets and apostles. Therefore, like the Christian religion itself, all the preaching of the Church must be nourished and ruled by sacred Scripture. For in the sacred books, the Father who is in heaven meets His children with great love and speaks with them; and the force and power in the word of God is so great that it remains the support and energy of the Church, the strength of faith for her sons, the food of the soul, the pure and perennial source of spiritual life."

Vatican II, Dogmatic Constitution on Divine Revelation, no. 21.

INTERPRETATION OF SACRED SCRIPTURE

"Since God speaks in sacred Scripture through men in human fashion, the interpreter of sacred Scripture, in order to see clearly what God wanted to communicate to us, should carefully investigate what meaning the sacred writers really intended, and what God wanted to manifest by means of their words.

"Those who search out the intention of the sacred writers must, among other things, have regard for 'literary forms.' For truth is proposed and expressed in a variety of ways, depending on whether a text is history of one kind or another, or whether its form is that of prophecy, poetry, or some other type of speech. The interpreter must investigate what meaning the sacred writer intended to express and actually expressed in particular circumstances as he used contemporary literary forms in accordance with the situation of his own time and culture. For the correct understanding of what the sacred author wanted to assert, due attention must be paid to the customary and characteristic styles of perceiving, speaking, and narrating which prevailed at the

time of the sacred writer, and to the customs men normally followed at that period in their everyday dealings with one another."
Vatican II, Dogmatic Constitution on Divine Revelation, no. 12.

Instructions

MATERIALS FOR THE STUDY

This Study Guide: The Gospel According to Luke

Bible: The New American Bible with Revised New Testament or The New Jerusalem Bible is recommended. Paraphrased editions are discouraged as they offer little if any help when facing difficult textual questions. Choose a Bible you feel free to write in or underline.

Commentary: The Collegeville Bible Commentary: New Testament Series, volume 3, *The Gospel According to Luke* by Jerome Kodell, O.S.B., (The Liturgical Press) is used with this study. The abbreviation for this commentary, CBC-NT volume 3, and the assigned pages are found at the beginning of each lesson.

ADDITIONAL MATERIALS

Bible Dictionary: *The Dictionary of the Bible* by John L. McKenzie, (Macmillan) is highly recommended as an additional reference.

Notebook: A notebook may be useful for lecture notes and your personal reflections.

WEEKLY LESSONS

Lesson 1—Luke 1
Lesson 2—Luke 2
Lesson 3—Luke 3–5
Lesson 4—Luke 6–7
Lesson 5—Luke 8–9
Lesson 6—Luke 10–11
Lesson 7—Luke 12–13
Lesson 8—Luke 14–16
Lesson 9—Luke 17–19
Lesson 10—Luke 20–22
Lesson 11—Luke 23–24

YOUR DAILY PERSONAL STUDY

The first step is prayer. Open your heart and mind to God. Reading Scripture is an opportunity to listen to God who loves you. Pray that the same Holy Spirit who guided the formation of Scripture will inspire you to correctly understand what you read and empower you to make what you read a part of your life.

The next step is commitment. Daily spiritual food is as necessary as food for the body. This study is divided into daily units. Schedule a regular time and place for your study, as free from distractions as possible. Allow about twenty minutes a day. Make it a daily appointment with God.

As you begin each lesson read the assigned chapters of Scripture found at the beginning of each lesson, the footnotes in your Bible, and then the indicated pages of the commentary. This preparation will give you an overview of the entire lesson and help you to appreciate the context of individual passages.

As you reflect on Scripture, ask yourself these four questions:

1. *What does the Scripture passage say?*
   Read the passage slowly and reflectively. Use your imagination to picture the scene or enter into it.

2. *What does the Scripture passage mean?*
   Read the footnotes and the commentary to help you understand what the sacred writers intended and what God wanted to communicate by means of their words.

3. *What does the Scripture passage mean to me?*
   Meditate on the passage. God's Word is living and powerful. What is God saying to you today? How does the Scripture passage apply to your life today?

4. *What am I going to do about it?*
   Try to discover how God may be challenging you in this passage. An encounter with God contains a challenge to know God's will and follow it more closely in daily life.

THE QUESTIONS ASSIGNED FOR EACH DAY

Read the questions and references for each day. The questions are designed to help you listen to God's Word and to prepare you for the weekly small-group discussion.

Some of the questions can be answered briefly and objectively by referring to the Bible references and the commentary *(What does the passage say?)*. Some will lead you to a better understanding of how the Scriptures apply to the Church, sacraments, and society *(What does the passage mean?)*. Some questions will invite you to consider how God's Word challenges or supports you in your relationships with God and others *(What does the passage mean to me?)*. Finally, the questions will lead you to examine your actions in light of Scripture *(What am I going to do about it?)*.

Write your responses in this study guide or in a notebook to help you clarify and organize your thoughts and feelings.

THE WEEKLY SMALL-GROUP MEETING

The weekly small-group sharing is the heart of the Little Rock Scripture Study Program. Participants gather in small groups to share the results of praying, reading and reflecting on Scripture and on the assigned questions. The goal of the discussion is for group members to be strengthened and nourished individually and as a community through sharing how God's Word speaks to them and affects their daily lives. The daily study questions will guide the discussion; it is not necessary to discuss all the questions.

All members share the responsibility of creating an atmosphere of loving support and trust in the group by respecting the opinions and experiences of others, and by affirming and encouraging one another. The simple shared prayer which begins and ends each small group meeting also helps create the open and trusting environment in which group members can share their faith deeply and grow in the study of God's Word.

A distinctive feature of this program is its emphasis on and trust in God's presence working in and through each member. Sharing responses to God's presence in the Word and in others can bring about remarkable growth and transformation.

THE WRAP-UP LECTURE

The lecture is designed to develop and clarify the themes of the lesson. It is not intended to form the basis for the group discussion. For this reason the lecture is always held at the end of the meeting. If several small groups meet at one time, the large group will gather together in a central location to listen to the lecture.

Lectures may be given by a local speaker. They are also available on audio- or video-cassette.

LESSON 1 Luke 1
CBC-NT volume 3, pages 7–20

Day 1

1. How has Luke prepared for his task of writing this Gospel (1:1-4)?
2. How are you preparing for communicating the good news of Jesus in your life?
3. a) If you were writing a Gospel today, who would you want to address?
   b) What view of Jesus would you highlight?

Day 2

4. Where might a Gospel-writer get information about the life of Jesus today?
5. The earlier Gospel According to Mark had no stories of Jesus' birth and childhood. Why did Luke add the infancy section?
6. What makes Zechariah and Elizabeth appropriate models of Jews awaiting the fulfillment of God's promises (1:5-6)?

Day 3

7. From what you know of John the Baptist's later life, how was he like Elijah, the prophet (1:13-17)? (See 3:1-20; 9:7-9; 1 Kgs 17–19; Mal 3:23.)
8. a) Why is Zechariah punished (1:20)?
   b) What types of proof do you desire before believing?
9. Zechariah returned home only after his days of ministry were complete (1:23). What does this teach you about faithfulness?

Day 4

10. God demonstrates that Mary is the "favored one" by choosing her to bear Jesus (1:28-31). See the following passages to discover how others experienced God's favor: 1 Sam 2:21; Ps 85; Ps 128:1-4; Rom 1:5.

11. Read 1:38. Describe a situation where you could only repeat words like Mary's. (See 22:42; Gen 22:2-3; Rom 4:20-21.)

12. How is Mary similar to the ark of the covenant (1:40-41)? (See 2 Sam 6:2-16.)

Day 5

13. Compare Mary's prayer to that of Hannah, the mother of Samuel (1 Sam 1:1-24; 2:1-10). How are the situations of these two mothers similar or different?

14. a) What strikes you as the main theme of Mary's canticle?
    b) What seems to be a theme in your own prayer life?

15. What is significant about the circumstances surrounding Zechariah's restored gift of speech?

Day 6

16. How does Zechariah use his restored gift of speech (1:64)?

17. Which natural gifts are most likely to be taken for granted or misused?
    a) in general?
    b) in your own life?

18. Which verses of Zechariah's canticle (1:67-79) are the most comforting to you? Why?

LESSON 2 Luke 2

CBC-NT volume 3, pages 20–25

Day 1

1. What insight would you share from last week's discussion or lecture?
2. Why was it important for Joseph to be of the house of David (2:4)? (See 2 Sam 7:16; John 7:42; Rom 1:3.)
3. a) How will the empire of Caesar Augustus eventually be affected by the events in Nazareth and Bethlehem (2:1-5)? (See 3:1-2; Matt 28:18-20; Acts 1:8.)
   b) How have seemingly insignificant religious events had major effects on the world in our time?

Day 2

4. What is the significance of identifying Jesus as Mary's "firstborn son" (2:7)? (See Exod 13:15; Num 3:13; Deut 21:15-17.)
5. a) How do the shepherds reflect the "lowliness" described in the canticle of Mary (2:8-18)? (See 1:46-55.)
   b) Where do we find such lowliness in our world today?
6. About what things does the Lord tell us, "Do not be afraid" (2:10)?

Day 3

7. a) In what ways can Christians help the world accept God's gift of peace (2:14)? (See John 20:21.)
   b) How do you promote peace?
8. What characteristics did the shepherds demonstrate in 2:15-20?
9. Why does Simeon say that now he can be dismissed in peace (2:29-32)?

Day 4

10. How are the words of Simeon a prelude to Calvary (2:34-35)?
11. Why are Simeon and Anna able to recognize the Messiah when others do not (2:29-30, 37-38)? (See 1:6.)
12. What are some parallels between the infancy narratives of John the Baptist (Luke 1) and Jesus (Luke 2)?

Day 5

13. Which Old Testament figure is alluded to in the description of Jesus' growth (2:40)? (See 1 Sam 2:21, 26.)
14. What do you learn about Jesus' religious upbringing from the account found in 2:41-47?
15. What more important event is anticipated by Jesus' three days in the Temple (2:46)? (See 9:22.)

Day 6

16. What does Jesus' statement in 2:49 tell you about his identity? (See 10:21; 11:2-4.)
17. Jesus apparently had greater understanding than Joseph and Mary, yet he remained obedient (2:51). Why?

LESSON 3 Luke 3–5

CBC-NT volume 3, pages 25–37

Day 1

1. Which story or theme from Luke's infancy narrative (chapters 1–2) has been especially important to your understanding of Jesus?
2. a) What is your impression of John from 3:1-22 or other readings? (See Mark 6:17-29; John 1:19-34.)
   b) Is there anyone like him around today?
   c) In what ways can you imitate John the Baptist?
3. The verses John the Baptist quotes from Isaiah are used by the Church during Advent (3:3-6). How do they apply?

Day 2

4. How does one live as a true child of Abraham (3:8)? (See Sir 44:19-20; Rom 4:16; Jas 2:21-22.)
5. a) Is the message of John the Baptist as valid today as it was then (3:10-14)?
   b) What do you think John would instruct you to do?
6. What does it mean to be baptized in the Holy Spirit and in fire (3:16)? (See 12:49; Matt 3:11; Acts 1:5; 2:3.)

Day 3

7. a) Why does Luke publish the genealogy of Jesus after Jesus' baptism (3:23-38)?
   b) Unlike Matthew, Luke traces Jesus genealogy back to Adam. Why?
8. How would you describe the purpose of the devil's temptations of Jesus in the desert (4:1-12)? (See Gen 3:1-7; Acts 8:18-24.)
9. Which of the three temptations is most typical of your struggles?

Day 4

10. What evidence in 4:14-22 shows that Jesus was a faithful Jew? (See 13:10; 19:45-47; Mark 14:12-16.)

11. Why did Jesus' audience become angry (4:28)? (See 1 Kgs 17:9; 2 Kgs 5:14; Acts 13:44-49.)

12. a) Why is it often easier to listen to correction from afar than from someone near? (See John 1:46.)
    b) From whom especially is it difficult for you to accept correction?

Day 5

13. Why did Jesus not want the demons to identify him (4:41)? (See Mark 1:44-45; Acts 16:16-18.)

14. Simon responds to Jesus' command with faith (5:5). What has been a response of faith in your own life? (See 22:41-44; Gen 22:1-3.)

15. Why does Simon tell Jesus to depart (5:8)?

Day 6

16. a) To whose faith was Jesus responding in the healing of the paralytic (5:18-20)?
    b) What implications does this have for our prayer lives?

17. How can the sacrament of reconciliation be a source of healing (5:24)?

18. In what circumstances is Christian fasting valuable today (5:33-35)? (See Matt 6:16-18; Acts 13:2.)

LESSON 4 Luke 6–7

CBC-NT volume 3, pages 38–47

Day 1

1. What insight from last week's lesson has begun to enter your prayer life?
2. a) Why is a day set aside for the Lord (6:2)? (See Exod 20:8-11; Deut 5:14-15.)
   b) Is Jesus violating the Sabbath (6:1-5)?
3. What kind of activity is recommended on the Lord's Day (6:9)? (See Isa 58:13-14.)

Day 2

4. a) Why did Jesus spend the night in prayer (6:12-13)?
   b) What in your life would lead you to pray this way?
5. Compare the beatitudes in 6:20-26 with the beatitudes in Matt 5:1-12. What are the differences?
6. a) To which of the beatitudes do you feel most committed?
   b) What could you do to bring that beatitude to life?

Day 3

7. How is it possible to love one's enemies (6:27)? Can you think of any examples? (See Rom 12:9-21.)
8. a) How have you experienced God's compassion through another person (6:36)? (See 1 John 3:16.)
   b) How have you shared this compassion with someone else?
9. Can you think of times when blindness has prevented true understanding and forgiveness (6:41)? (See Rom 2:1; Gal 6:2-5.)

Day 4

10. How has attention to the Word of God affected your life (6:47-49)? (See 8:11-15; Heb 4:12.)

11. What is the significance of Jesus ministering to the centurion's servant (7:1-10)? (See Acts 10:34-35; 1 Cor 12:13.)

12. What is the difference between the raising of the widow's son and the resurrection of Jesus (7:11-15)? (See Rom 6:8-10; 1 Cor 15:3-5.)

Day 5

13. How does Jesus' answer to John's disciples confirm who he is (7:20-22)? (See 4:18-19; Isa 61:1-3.)

14. Explain 7:28. (See Rom 8:14-17.)

15. a) What are some current excuses for not practicing one's faith (7:31-35)?
    b) What are some of the ways to invite others back to full participation in faith?

Day 6

16. What is daring about the woman's action (7:37-38)? (See Matt 15:28; Acts 20:22-24; Phil 1:20-21.)

17. How does Jesus show that he knows both the woman and Simon (7:39-50)? (See John 2:24-25; Heb 4:12.)

18. How does the saying of Jesus in 7:47 apply to your own life? (See 6:36-38.)

LESSON 5 Luke 8–9

CBC-NT volume 3, pages 47–58

Day 1

1. What teaching of Jesus found in last week's lesson presents the greatest challenge to you?
2. After reading 8:1-3, what would be the appropriate response for someone who has experienced God's action in his or her life? (See 19:1-10; Exod 15:1; 1 John 4:11.)
3. Interpreting the seed as "opportunity to do good" (8:5-8), give examples of its application in the parable.

Day 2

4. In what ways are you preparing the "soil" of your life to receive the Word (8:15)? (See Isa 55:10-11; Mark 4:26-29.)
5. In what situations might it advance the Gospel to make good works public (8:16-17)? (See Ps 139:16; Matt 5:14-16; 6:1-16.)
6. The early Church Fathers often referred to the Church as a boat on stormy seas (8:22-25). What are some of the worst storms it has weathered? (See Acts 27:39-44; 1 Pet 3:19-21.)

Day 3

7. a) What evidence do you see today of demonic influence (8:27)?
   b) How does one combat evil? (See Acts 19:11-17; Eph 6:10-18; 1 Pet 5:8-11.)
8. Why does the Church warn against magical games and dabbling in the occult? (See 1 Sam 28:3-25; Acts 19:18-19.)
9. a) Why was the man not allowed to go with Jesus (8:38-39)?
   b) What has been the Lord's mandate to you?

Day 4

10. What is Luke's purpose in relating the conversation between Jesus and the healed woman (8:47-48)?

11. In what ways do you see the healing ministry of Jesus and the apostles continued in the Church today?

12. Why are the apostles told to take nothing along (9:3)? (See 10:4.)

Day 5

13. a) How did Jesus find private time with God (9:10, 18)?
    b) Are you able to find private time with Jesus? (See 6:12; Mark 1:35.)

14. What are some differences between Jesus' instructions for discipleship and contemporary notions of success (9:22-25)? (See Phil 2:5-11; Heb 5:8-10.)

15. Recall one of your own "mountaintop" experiences (9:28-36). What did you learn about yourself and God in this experience? (See Exod 19:3-5.)

Day 6

16. How has your faith been deepened through official ecumenical events or through personal sharing with those who are not Catholic (9:49-50)? (See 1 Tim 2:1-5.)

17. What did the journey to Jerusalem (9:51) mean for Jesus? (See 9:44-45; 18:31-34.)

18. What have you had to leave behind because of following Jesus toward Jerusalem (9:57-62)? (See Rom 6:1-11; 1 Cor 13:1-8.)

LESSON 6 Luke 10–11
CBC-NT volume 3, pages 58–67

Day 1

1. What insight would you share from last week's study or lecture?
2. a) Who are some of the laborers in our time (10:2)?
   b) In what ways are you asked to join the laborers?
3. Why will Sodom's judgment be less severe than that on Peter's hometown (10:12-13)? (See John 1:44-45.)

Day 2

4. What responsibility is placed upon you in the words of Jesus in 10:16? (See Rom 1:8; 1 Thess 1:6-8.)
5. What is the truth revealed by God to the childlike (10:21-24)? (See 1 Cor 2:14.)
6. What are the questions or concerns that expand or test your faith (10:25)?

Day 3

7. Read the Great Commandment in 10:27. How would you explain to a child the first part of the command?
8. a) Why would Jesus' Jewish listeners have been shocked by the Samaritan's action (10:31-35)?
   b) What type of person today would be a shock to you in that role?
9. How has Mary "chosen the better part" (10:42)?

Day 4

10. How do the stories of the Samaritan and the two women complement one another? (See 1 John 4:21.)
11. Which petition of the Lord's Prayer is the most meaningful to you (11:2-4)? Why? (See Matt 6:9-13.)
12. a) Summarize the message of these two parables about prayer (11:5-13.)
    b) Describe a time when you asked God for a greater outpouring of the Holy Spirit in your life (11:13.)

Day 5

13. Can you describe a situation that illustrates the truth of the saying in 11:17? (See 1 Cor 11:17-22.)
14. a) What does 11:28 mean to you? (See 8:21.)
    b) How might Jesus' words in 11:28 be interpreted as praise of his mother? (See 1:38, 45.)
15. How can an individual guard the light which is spoken of in 11:34-36?

Day 6

16. From an ordinary day, name two uses of sight that promote inner light and two that promote inner darkness.
17. What do you believe most angered the "scholars of the law" in Jesus' comments to them (11:45-54)?

LESSON 7 Luke 12–13

CBC-NT volume 3, pages 67–75

Day 1

1. In the last several weeks what have you learned about Jesus from Luke's portrayal of him?
2. a) What is comforting about Jesus' words in 12:2?
   b) What is disturbing about his words? (See Eccl 10:20.)
3. Recall and describe an instance when you experienced God's loving care in your life (12:6-7). (See 12:28-32.)

Day 2

4. Why does Jesus speak so strongly about blaspheming against the Holy Spirit (12:10)? (See Matt 12:31-32; Mark 3:28-30.)
5. a) What forms of greed are there besides greed for money and possessions (12:15)?
   b) How can greed be transformed into generosity? (See Gal 5:22-23; Heb 13:16; 1 Pet 4:9-10.)
6. There are strong warnings against wealth found in the Bible. (See 12:20-21; Matt 19:23-26; Rev 3:17-18.) What is the danger of wealth?

Day 3

7. a) What are the main worries which threaten your peace of mind?
   b) Why is it difficult to trust Jesus' promise in 12:22-31?
8. Think back over the past week and recall times when you were called to seek God's kingdom first (12:31). List these times.
9. The parable of 12:35-40 encourages a spirit of readiness for the Lord's coming. In what ways can this readiness be demonstrated in your life? (See Matt 24:36-44.)

Day 4

10. What are the gifts especially entrusted to you (12:48)? (See Rom 12:6-8; 1 Cor 12:4-11.)

11. Read the following passages: Exod 13:21; Ps 17:3; Isa 43:2; Acts 2:1-4. How does the use of fire in these passages help you understand Jesus' saying in 12:49?

12. How can you reconcile Jesus' title as Prince of Peace with the words in 12:51? (See Isa 9:5.)

Day 5

13. What challenges are faced by families who do not share a common faith in Jesus (12:52-53)?

14. What are some of the signs of the kingdom in the world today (12:54-56)? (See 1 Cor 13:1-7; Col 3:12-17.)

15. Based on the examples given in 13:1-5, what is Jesus saying about appearances and true spiritual goodness? (See Matt 7:21.)

Day 6

16. a) Why was the chief of the synagogue angry at Jesus (13:14)?
    b) In what situations have you seen anger today when good is done?

17. a) How might today's Church leaders be intimidated in exercising their mission (13:31-33)? (See Jer 38:1-13.)
    b) Can you mention any examples of courage under this intimidation?

18. What might prevent you from entering the narrow gate (13:23-24)? (See Matt 7:21; Eph 5:1-5; Col 3:5-17.)

LESSON 8 Luke 14–16

CBC-NT volume 3, pages 75–86

Day 1

1. What new awareness about the kingdom of God did you gain from last week's lesson?
2. a) How does the healing of the man with dropsy (14:1-6) demonstrate the kingdom of God to you?
   b) What is Jesus' response to the scrutiny of the Pharisees (14:1-6)? (See Mark 3:2-5.)
3. a) What is the difference between true and false humility (14:10-11)? (See 18:9-14; Sir 3:18; Matt 11:29.)
   b) Give an example of the humility Jesus speaks of in the parable.

Day 2

4. a) Who are the poor and the outcast in your midst (14:12-14)?
   b) How can Jesus' instructions to invite them to the banquet be made practical today?
5. The invited guests were doing good things at the wrong time (14:18-20). (See Prov 3:6.) What are some excuses we use to decline God's invitation?
6. How can one legitimately hate or turn away from family and self (14:26)? (See Rom 6:6-11.)

Day 3

7. Jesus uses a simile about salt to speak about discipleship (14:34-35). Read the way this image is used in Matt 5:13 and in Mark 9:40 and describe ways you are challenged to be salt in your community.
8. Why is there more rejoicing over the repentant sinner than over the righteous (15:7, 10)? (See Ezek 33:11-19.)
9. In what ways are both sons in the parable "lost" or "prodigal" (5:11-32)?

Day 4

10. In what ways can the young son's journey be symbolic of every Christian's spiritual journey (15:11-21)? (See 19:1-10; Acts 9:1-19.)
11. The father required no proof of repentance (15:21-22). What does this teach about love and forgiveness? (See Hos 11:9.)
12. What is an offense you have special difficulty forgiving?

Day 5

13. In what ways are you able to identify with the older son (15:25-32)?
14. Read Jesus' story of the dishonest steward (6:1-8).
    a) Give a modern example of industriousness motivated by worldly concerns.
    b) Give a modern example of "acting prudently" for the kingdom of God (16:8). (See Matt 6:19-21.)
15. Share a story that illustrates the truth of 16:10.

Day 6

16. a) What is it about material goods that threatens devotion to God (16:13)? (See Matt 6:25-31.)
    b) What steps do you take to ensure an appropriate Christian relationship to material goods?
17. The Church maintains the sacredness of marriage as reflecting God's relationship with the Church (16:18). (See Eph 5:25-33.) Considering the reality of divorce, how can we better support those in our parish families who are experiencing discord in their marriages?
18. What prevents people from believing in Christ (16:31)? (See Rom 10:14, 17; 1 Pet 2:11-12.)

LESSON 9 Luke 17–19

CBC-NT volume 3, pages 86–100

Day 1

1. Which parable in last week's lesson offered you new insights about faith?
2. What concerns do you have about setting a good example or being a good role model for others (17:1-2)? (See Prov 28:10.)
3. What opportunities has the Lord given you to increase your faith (17:5)? (See Phil 1:6; 2 Thess 1:3; 1 Pet 1:6-7.)

Day 2

4. a) Why are the lepers told to show themselves to the priests (17:14)? (See Lev 14:1-4; Mark 1:43-44.)
   b) To whom can you better relate, the one leper who returned to Jesus or the remaining nine?
5. How do the words of Jesus in 17:20-21 relate to the prayer he taught his disciples found in Matthew 6:10?
6. How would you summarize the teaching of Jesus in 17:22-37?

Day 3

7. What was the mistake of Lot's wife (17:32-33)? (See Gen 19:26.)
8. Use 17:33 as the basis of prayer. In what way can one lose his or her life? (See Matt 10:39; 16:24-25; John 10:25.)
9. Imagine the scene between the widow and the judge (18:1-5). Can you describe a time when you were as persistent as the widow?

Day 4

10. Is the Pharisee or the tax collector most like yourself (18:9-14)? In what ways?
11. What are the qualities of a child that would promote openness to the kingdom of God (18:17)? (See Ps 131:1-3; Matt 18:2-3.)
12. Explain Jesus' question in 18:19. (See Matt 19:17.)

Day 5

13. Jesus refers to the commandments (18:20). Which are the most challenging for you, the "spiritual" (Exod 20:2-8) or the "social" (Exod 20:12-17)?
14. Describe a situation that demonstrates the truth of 18:27.
15. What common qualities are possessed by the blind beggar (18:35-43) and Zacchaeus (19:1-10)?

Day 6

16. What did Jesus indicate by riding on an ass (19:33-35)? (See Zech 9:9-10.)
17. What attempts to silence Jesus' disciples are made today (19:39-40)?
18. In what ways is the Church in our day called to a "cleansing" (19:45-46)? (See Mal 3:1-3.)

LESSON 10 Luke 20–22

CBC-NT volume 3, pages 100–113

Day 1

1. Which character from last week's lesson is a model of faith for you?
2. At what times have you experienced the authority of God in your life (20:1-8)? (See Acts 4:19-20.)
3. Why are the religious officials threatened by the parable told by Jesus (20:19)? (See 16:14-15; Matt 23:1-7; Mark 12:38-40.)

Day 2

4. Is it ever morally right to refuse paying taxes (20:25)? (See 1 Macc 13:39; Matt 17:25-27; Rom 13:6.)
5. a) Why did Mosaic law require a man to marry his brother's widow (20:28)? (See Deut 25:5-10.)
   b) How does Jesus' response (20:35-38) redirect their question?
6. How do we reflect in our daily lives that we are children of God or children of the resurrection (20:36)?

Day 3

7. Comment on the saying: "A person is rich in proportion to the things he or she can leave alone" (21:1-4). (See 12:27-32; Rev 2:9.)
8. What makes people vulnerable to false prophets and their messages (21:8-9)? (See Matt 7:15-16; 24:11-13; 2 Cor 11:12-13.)
9. a) Who are some Christian martyrs of this century (21:16)?
   b) What is the greatest test of your own "perseverance" (21:19)? (See Isa 40:31; Heb 10:36-39.)

Day 4

10. What is indicated by the "times of the Gentiles" (21:24)? (See Rom 11:11-15.)
11. a) What is the reign of God?
    b) Is the reign of God near now (21:31)? (See 17:20-21.)
12. What prevents people from experiencing the reign of God (21:34-36)? (See Mark 14:35; Rom 10:14-17.)

Day 5

13. In this Gospel, Satan attacked Jesus and others by temptation (4:1-12), in physical ways (4:41), and through the agency of other people (22:3). How does Satan work today?
14. How is the Eucharist (the Mass) a remembrance of Jesus (22:19)? (See Exod 12:14; John 6:51-58; 1 Cor 10:16-17; 11:24-26.)
15. How do you feel toward Judas (22:21-22, 47-48)? (See Matt 27:3-10.)

Day 6

16. Why was Peter not disqualified from leadership by his denials (22:31-32)? (See 22:54-62.)
17. Explain Jesus' reply "It is enough!" in 22:38 and "Stop, no more of this!" in 22:51.
18. Recall a time when you prayed like Jesus (22:42). How did you get through the difficulty?

LESSON 11 Luke 23–24
CBC-NT volume 3, pages 113–124

Day 1

1. What insight from last week's lesson has helped you better understand discipleship?
2. Why didn't Jesus want to admit the name "Messiah" (23:2-3)? (See Mark 8:29-30; John 6:15.)
3. What united Herod and Pilate in friendship (23:12)? (See 13:31; Acts 4:27.)

Day 2

4. a) What was the pressure that made Pilate hand Jesus over (23:22-25)?
   b) Give an example of this type of pressure today and how it could be resisted.
5. Read the proverb in 23:31.
   a) How does this apply to Jesus?
   b) Are there applications in the Church today?
6. What information in chapters 22–23 demonstrates that Jesus, though falsely accused, freely gave himself in his passion and death? (See 22:15, 19-20, 42; 23:34-36, 43, 46.)

Day 3

7. a) Why did the two thieves respond so differently to Jesus (23:39-43)?
   b) How is this passage a source of hope? (See Matt 20:1-16.)
8. What is symbolized by the tearing of the sanctuary curtain (23:45)? (See Exod 26:31-33; Heb 6:19; 10:19-20.)
9. a) What risk did Joseph take in burying Jesus (23:50-53)? (See John 7:45-52.)
   b) What similar risk might you be called to take in your own life?

Day 4

10. How did it happen that women were the first witnesses instead of the apostles (24:1-5)? (See Mark 16:1-8.)

11. a) Why did the story of the women seem like nonsense (24:11)?
    b) Describe a time when you reacted to apparent nonsense as Peter did (24:12).

12. What purpose could Jesus have in asking the disciples about what he already knew (24:17)?

Day 5

13. What similarities do you see between Jesus teaching in 24:27 and what is reported about him in 2:46-47?

14. What experiences have you had that opened your eyes to the presence of Jesus in your midst (24:30-31)?

15. When or how have the Scriptures spoken most powerfully to you (24:37)? (See 2 Kgs 23:1-3; Heb 4:12.)

Day 6

16. a) What is the "promise" of the Father which will come from on high (24:49)? (See Ezek 36:27; Joel 3:1-2; Acts 1:8; 2:33.)
    b) How have you experienced this promise in your life?

17. What brings you great joy as a Christian (24:52)?

18. How do you think the study of this Gospel will affect your relationship to Jesus, and your relationship to others?

NOTES